BY THIS TIME TOMORROW

....

Uncommon Faith-Filled Words and Prophetic Declarations That Will Change Your Life Forever

....

By:

DANIEL C. OKPARA

Looking for resources to keep your spirit on fire?

Follow me on Facebook for a daily 30-minute morning broadcast. Stir your spirit for Jesus every morning and every night. Start and end your day with powerful prayers and teachings and command your breakthrough.

<u>**JOIN NOW FOR FREE**</u>

https://www.facebook.com/drdanielokpara/

Copyright © March 2020 by Daniel C. Okpara.

All Rights Reserved. Please do not copy or share any part of this book without the written consent of the author or his representative. Small excerpts may be quoted and used in critical reviews, Bible study groups, or fellowships.

TO EDIFY, HEAL, AND BLESS

The author provides the content of this book in good faith: to enlighten, encourage, and heal. He believes that when the subject discussed is followed, it will produce healing, divine intervention, and miracles from God. However, he does not intend his revelations to take the place of professional counseling and suggestions in your life. Neither is the teaching in this book supposed to be a doctrine to alter your faith in Christ. The author is sure and believes you will be blessed reading this book. However, he will bear no responsibility for any adverse consequences from any wrong understanding and application of the subject taught in this material. He prays, though, that you will make good use of the teaching and increase your faith in God.

Published By:

Better Life Media.

BETTER LIFE WORLD OUTREACH CENTER.

Website: www.BetterLifeWorld.org

Email: info@betterlifeworld.org

FOLLOW US ON FACEBOOK

Like our Page on Facebook for updates:

www.facebook.com/drdanielokpara

This title and others are available for quantity discounts for sale promotions, gifts, and evangelism. Visit our website or email us to get started.

Any scripture quotation in this book is taken from the King James Version, New King James Version, and New International Version, except where stated—used by permission.

All texts, calls, letters, testimonies, and inquiries are welcome.

BE EMPOWERED ON SOCIAL MEDIA

Day 235 of 365

Today, God says...

"He has begun a good work in your life, and He will bring it to perfection. He will not abandon you half way. Yes, you have had problems, drawbacks, challenges, and red sea situations, but He will see you through. Your setback is temporary. It is a setup for God's work in your life. Only believe. Everything about you will end in praise."

DR. DANIEL OKPARA | WORD4TODAY | DAY 235

Are you looking for resources to keep your spirit on fire? Who says you can't use social media and also keep your spirit healthy for God?

Follow me on Facebook for powerful daily broadcasts and prayers to stir your spirit for Jesus every day and command your breakthrough.

www.facebook.com/drdanielokpara

RECEIVE WEEKLY PRAYERS

Powerful Prayers Sent to Your Inbox Every Monday

Enter your email address to receive notifications of new posts, prayers and prophetic declarations sent to you by email.

Email Address

Sign Me Up

Go to breakthroughprayers to subscribe to receive free weekly prayer points and prophetic declarations sent to you by email.

www.breakthroughprayers.org

FREE BOOKS

Thank you for obtaining this book. Here are four powerful books today for free. Download them on our website and take your relationship with God to a new level.

www.betterlifeworld.org/grow

CONTENTS

BE EMPOWERED ON SOCIAL MEDIA 5

RECEIVE WEEKLY PRAYERS 6

FREE BOOKS 7

OPENING DECLARATION 10

MY MISSION: WHY I WRITE 11

INTRODUCTION: YOU RULE WITH WORDS 12

1: THE MYSTERY OF WORD SEEDS: WHAT YOU SAY IS WHAT YOU REAP 20

2: YOU WILL DECREE A THING; THAT IS, YOU, NOT SOMEONE ELSE .44

3: THE DIFFERENCE BETWEEN POSITIVE CONFESSION AND PROPHETIC DECLARATION 53

4: BY THIS TIME TOMORROW 65

5: SPEAK TO THE MOUNTAIN, NOT ABOUT IT 85

6: SPEAK TO THE STORM; DON'T LET IT SPEAK TO YOU 95

7: DON'T BURY THE CHILD YET 113

8: HEALING WORDS TO COMMAND YOUR HEALTH 129

9: BANISH ANXIETY, WORRY, AND DEPRESSION 142

10: FAVOR WORDS 146

11: DECLARATIONS OVER YOUR FINANCES 153

12: DECLARATIONS OVER YOUR MIND 159

13: DECLARATIONS OVER YOUR LIFE 170

GET IN TOUCH 182

BOOKS BY THE SAME AUTHOR 183

ABOUT THE AUTHOR 187

NOTES 189

OPENING DECLARATION

My help comes from the Lord, which made heaven and earth. He will not allow my foot to be moved.

Behold, he that keeps me shall neither slumber nor sleep.

The Lord is my keeper: the Lord is my shade upon my right hand.

The sun shall not strike me by day, nor the moon by night.

The Lord shall preserve me from all evil: he shall protect my soul.

The Lord shall protect my going out and my coming in from this time forth, and even forevermore.

MY MISSION: WHY I WRITE

God spoke to me in 1998 to write down the things He shows me, that in time, He would use them to set the captives free. I was twenty-one years old then, and that was when I started writing down whatever God showed me in His Word, visions, and dreams.

To the glory of God, we have received thousands of testimonies of salvation, deliverance, and mysterious divine encounters through the books we publish and send out to the world.

So writing is a divine mandate for me. Therefore, as you read this book and others, expect God's power to manifest beyond your imagination and set you free. You will be empowered to move into your testimony.

INTRODUCTION: YOU RULE WITH WORDS

"Man is created to create. And one way we can use God's ability in us to create is by the way we speak."

Words are spiritual forces that have the power to create physical realities. By speaking a certain way, you can fast-track the manifestation of your miracles and change your world very quickly.

Your words create your world.

Have you ever asked yourself, "How does man resemble God? The scripture says that man was created in God's image, so how do we resemble Him?"

I'm sure you know that we do not look like God in the same way a son would look like the dad or a daughter like the mum? Our resemblance of God is not in our physical qualities but in our creative abilities.

When God says, "Hey, I made you in my image. You look like me." He does not mean how fair or how dark you are. He means that you can do what He did. You have His kind of ability in you.

God is not white, neither is He black. He is God, and there is no way to describe His appearance. Those who attempted it in scriptures couldn't do that. They ended up describing Him as an immeasurable, massive, immense, inexpressible amount of Light.

So we do not look like God with the way we appear, but with His ability in us to do what He can do.

Man is created to create. And one way we can use God's ability in us to create is by the way we speak.

God created the entire universe with His words, and while creating man, He said:

> Let Us make man in Our image, according to Our likeness; let them have dominion over the fish of the sea, over the birds of the air, and over the cattle, over all the earth and over every creeping thing that creeps on the earth - Gen. 1:26.

God's purpose for creating man is to have dominion, replenish, be fruitful and multiply.

But notice that the first assignment man executed involved the use of his words. The Bible says:

"God formed every beast of the field and every fowl of the air, and brought them unto Adam to see what he would call them; and whatsoever Adam called every living creature, that was the name thereof." - Genesis 2:19

This means that whether the man He made would create or not depended on his use of words. Whether he will be fruitful, and multiply, and replenish the earth, and subdue it, and have dominion over the fish of the sea, and over the fowl of the air, and over every living thing that moves upon the earth, depends on what he says or didn't say.

You can never dominate and rule your world if you don't know the power of what you say. Your words are what create your world.

The world was created by God with His Words. You have the power to create and recreate your own world with your words. When we learn to speak like God, we will begin to manifest the divine, and all that concerns us will change dramatically, we will begin to prevail in our daily events.

THE MYSTERY OF NAMING

Did you notice that whatever you called your child is what it bears, and that is what it grows to be called? It's called naming.

Have you ever sat down to wonder how a dog can answer an owner by the name the owner gave it? The same dog will answer this name when others call it by that name. It's the power of words. Whatever you call your pet is what it answers.

Words give names, and these names stay that way forever. Even in the book of life, God records your name by the name you were given or the one you chose to be called.

Isn't that interesting? God calls you by the name you were called here on earth, which you accepted to answer.

NAME YOUR PROBLEM

Your deliverance and breakthrough start from here: Name your problem.

I know. The doctor says it's cancer, anxiety neurosis, or whatever. But what do you call the problem?

They said you are weak, and you won't amount to anything. But what do you say? Give your problem a name that belittles it and shows it's not what it is. The name you call your problem is what it will answer.

In this book, I will take you on a journey to change your world by the power of faith-filled words and prophetic declarations. From chapter one to chapter seven, we will uncover scriptures that will show you the power of speaking to your life with faith-filled words. Then from chapter eight to the last chapter (thirteen), you will see compelling examples of prophetic words and faith declarations that will change your life. Memorize and declare them day in day out. Give yourself a personal assignment to use these powerful words to reprogram your today and tomorrow. Expect an unusual encounter as you read this book.

"You can never dominate and rule your world if you don't know the power of what you say. Your words are what creates your world."

1

THE MYSTERY OF WORD SEEDS: WHAT YOU SAY IS WHAT YOU REAP

"A man will be satisfied with good by the fruit of his mouth, and the recompense of a man's hands will be rendered to him." – Proverbs 12:14

You've heard the saying, "You'll reap what you sow!"

That's an eternal truth.

However, when we hear that statement, we often think more of our actions. Interestingly, words are also seeds, and they bear corresponding fruits.

In today's opening verse, the writer compared words with work. The same way you get rewarded for the works of your hands is the same way you will be rewarded for the words of your mouth. In fact, your word seeds influence your work fruits.

YOUR WORDS INFLUENCE YOUR WORK AND PRAYER SEEDS

Prayer and work are like seeds. When you pray and work, you are likened to someone who plants seeds in their vineyard. But you need to water these seeds for the seeds to produce their intended fruits.

Kind words, positive words, Bible-based words are the manure that nurtures your prayer and work seeds and empowers them to produce good fruits. While negative words, fear-filled and hostile words are weeds that choke your prayer and work seeds and prevent them from yielding the proper fruits for you.

> *"Negative, fearful words cancel the effectiveness of your prayer and work."*

The writer of Proverbs goes on to say the same thing in another place to underscore the importance of this principle:

> A man's stomach will be satisfied with the fruit of his mouth; he will be satisfied with the consequence of his words. (Prov. 18:20 - TLB)

Your words produce fruits that fill your belly. If they are the right words, faith words, and scripture words, the results are great peace, progress, and health. But if they are wrong words, hating words, fearful words, death words, then the results are confusion, stagnation, and sickness.

You do not attract spiritual sympathy by looking helpless and talking like someone without hope. Humans may feel for you when you act and speak like that, but human pity does not permanently solve your problem.

So, which is better? That people sympathized with you and threw some leftovers at you in the name of kindness, or that God's power manifested and opened the heavens of favor, mercy, and blessings for you? I think you'd be better with the latter.

Don't talk to attract human pity without recourse to God's word for your life. You should say what God says about you and lose people's pity rather than draw their sympathy and delay God's mercy and intervention.

> *"Stop saying what people want to hear. Start saying what God will do."*

End all forms of pity-party. Self-damaging and self-deflating words have direct consequences in your life.

THEIR WORDS LED TO THEIR DEATH

Twelve people went to spy the land of Canaan. On their return, ten of them said, "Look, the land is beautiful. We love it, but we can't enter the land. There are giants there who look very big and dominating. They'll kill us all if we dare."

They convinced the rest of the multitude, and they cried, "We wish we had died in Egypt or even here in the wilderness, rather than be taken into this country ahead of us. Jehovah will kill us there, and our wives and little ones will become slaves. Let's get out of here and return to Egypt!" The idea swept the camp. "Let's elect a leader to take us back to Egypt!" they shouted." (Numbers 14:2-4 - TLB).

They forgot everything God had done for them in the past and believed more in their enemies' ability. Only two of the twelve, Joshua and Caleb, said, "It is a wonderful country ahead, and the Lord loves us. He will bring us safely into the land and give it to us. It is very fertile, a land 'flowing with milk and honey'! Do not rebel against the Lord, and do not fear the people of the land, for they are but bread for us to eat! The Lord is with us, and he has removed his protection from them! Don't be afraid of them! (Vs. 7-9)."

Moses prayed, and God answered and said,

Say to them, 'As I live,' says the Lord, 'Just as you have spoken in My hearing, so I will do to you (vs. 28).

Bible history tells us that all those people died in the wilderness except Joshua and Caleb. They didn't see the land; only their children did. Why? Because they said they wouldn't see the land because of the giants, and God answered them according to their words. They sowed word seeds of fear, discouragement, death, and failure, and that's what they reaped in their realities.

When we speak fear instead of faith, what we are doing is believing that the enemy is more powerful than our Creator, who says He is with us.

Words are powerful seeds that bear corresponding fruits. If you say you're going to die or that you're dying, God says, "Okay, that's what will happen."

If you say, "I'm finished. This is it. I'm not coming out of this." God says, "Okay, let it be done to you according to your words."

TRANSFORM YOUR LIFE WITH WORDS

The Word of God is a seed. Start planting it today for your health, breakthrough, protection, victory, and supernatural connection.

> 26 Then Jesus said, "God's kingdom is like a man who plants seed in the ground. 27 The seed begins to grow. It grows night and day. It doesn't matter whether the man is sleeping or awake; the seed still grows. He doesn't know how it happens. 28 Without any help, the ground produces grain. First, the plant grows, then the head, and then all the grain in the head. 29 When the grain is ready, the man cuts it. This is the harvest time." – Mark 4:26-29 (ERV)

When I read this scripture recently, I began to see why some of the things occurring in my life and ministry today are happening. We planted great word seeds in the past. When we didn't look like it, we kept speaking about how God would use our messages to touch lives globally. When we didn't even have two square meals a day, we spoke of how we would feed the poor, sponsor gospel meetings from community to community, and share thousands of free, soul-saving books in every nation.

A few times, some concerned friends tried to tell us to face reality. Other times, less friendly folks thought we were just overzealous and extreme with these things. But we kept speaking in season and out of season.

And those seeds were growing, even when we didn't know it; they were growing even when we thought we were not going to become those things again; they were growing even when we slept a few times along the way, and even when we tried to run away from the ministry. The seeds kept growing.

Today, Shining Light Christian Centre, Lagos, and Better Life World Outreach, our church and evangelism platforms, though only a few years, have touched lives in almost every part of the world. We share free food to hundreds of needy families every month, rehabilitate and train youths in skills, support small scale business people with money, distribute thousands of free books every month, online and offline, and more importantly, share the Gospel of Christ's love and deliverance with many every week.

The word seeds grew, and we're now seeing the significant impact in people's lives; we're now seeing results that make even us marvel. And we know it will only get better.

You can start the process of transforming your life today by what you say. Start planting the right word seeds and watch them grow. You may not feel the impact today, but every word seed you plant will yield corresponding fruit.

Instead of saying how bad things are, start saying that:

- Things are getting better.

- God is at work in my life.

- Everything about me is getting better

- My health is getting better

- My marriage is getting better

- My husband/wife is a great person

- I love more and more, every day

- I am loved more and more every day.

- I will not labor in vain.

- I hear the voice of God every day, and I am walking in His direction for my life

- I live in abundance.

- When others are saying there's a casting down, I will be saying there's a lifting up

- My finances are getting better

- I am coming out of debt

- My children will be taught of the Lord, and great shall be their peace.

Start sowing the right word seeds about your life and family from this day on. Practice memorizing some of these confessions and say them before the mirror every morning.

The chances are that your present circumstances result from the combination of your word-seeds, thought-seeds, and action-seeds. If you don't like what's happening today, change your seeds – beginning with your thought and word seeds.

> *"Your transformation is not too far away. It is right there in your mouth. Start using it now."*

I once said that your tongue is the president and secretary of your entire life. What it says is what happens to you.

So if you don't like where you are now and what is happening, start your transformation by sowing the right Bible-based word seeds.

WHAT HAPPENS WITH YOUR WORDS?

Speaking confidently and declaring God's promises, even during difficulties and pains, is a powerful weapon for our daily triumphs. It will bring you victory always – no matter how bad things may appear.

Here are some things that happen when we continue to declare God's Words and promises in faith over our lives.

1. We Encourage Ourselves

In life, there are times when our situations are best understood by us only. Things would look so messed up that even our closest friends would not fully understand how to help.

When we seem exhausted with circumstances, one thing that can encourage us is declaring what God has said. As we speak the WORD to ourselves and claim it, we'll somehow find encouragement and strength to face what's happening and overcome it.

2. We Create and Re-Create Our Experiences

The Word of God has creative powers. As we declare the WORDS in faith, those words create the realities we claim overtime.

This doesn't have anything to do with how you feel. Our relationship with God is not based and judged on feelings. I may be feeling awful and unspiritual, but it doesn't change the authenticity of what I declare. Sometimes, my feelings make it look like my prayers and declarations aren't getting above the ceiling. Sometimes, I may feel that I need to shout more or look more spiritual. But in reality, those are what they are – feelings.

> *The way you feel doesn't have anything to do with the Word of God. The WORD still works despite your feelings.*

Don't let your feelings decide how you handle the WORD. Let the WORD take care of how you feel

3. The Word Gives Life and Scares Death

The scripture says that "our words can get us killed or get us to live."

As we consistently declare the WORD, we invoke the life of God and scare death away.

> **Proverbs 15:4 (AMP):** A soothing tongue [speaking words that build up and encourage] is a tree of life, but a perverse tongue [speaking words that overwhelm and depress] crushes the spirit.

> **1 Peter 3:10 (AMP):** For the one who wants to enjoy life and see good days [good—whether apparent or not], must keep his tongue free from evil and his lips from speaking guile (treachery, deceit).

4. Justified or Condemned

Jesus said in Matthew 12:37,

> "For by thy words thou shalt be justified, and by thy words, thou shalt be condemned."

The word **_Justified_** is *dikaiósis* in Greek. It is the same word used in the law court to declare someone completely free and absolved of any offense. It means:

- To render righteous or such he ought to be.

- To show, exhibit, make clear, one to be righteous, such as he is and wishes himself to be considered.

- To declare, pronounce, one to be just, righteous.

- To set one free from all accusations.

While the word **_condemned_** is from the original Greek word *katadikazō,* which means to:

- To give judgment against one, to pronounce guilty.
- To condemn.
- To declare someone guilty of an offense and accusation.
- To imprison someone

Jesus is saying that it is from what you say that you will be either guilty as the devil accuses you and imprisoned, or be free from all accusations and live a free life. That is why we need to always declare God's promises instead of our fears.

5. God Will Do What He Hears You Say

That's what He says. Do you believe Him? If you truly know and believe that God will do what you say, what will you say? If you believe that God will do what He hears you say about your health, about your spouse, about your children, about your career and business, what will you say?

We often say that we believe, but our response and actions prove otherwise. If you believe that God will do what you say, then make what you say something good.

When we make positive declarations of faith, we do not deny the facts on the ground. Instead, we are confronting the realities with God's Words. We are giving angels the materials to work with for our lives. The words you declare will produce victory, protection, healing, and a continual breakthrough for you or the reverse.

BE MINDFUL OF YOUR WORDS

Always consider the impact of your words on others. Your comments can build you and others; they can also destroy you and others. The Bible says:

> Be gracious in your speech. The goal is to bring out the best in others in a conversation, not put them down, not cut them out (Col 4:6 - MSG)

Words can bring healing or destroy lives. To be mindful of your words to others, and to be constantly aware of the power that your words command is a powerful way to practice generosity.

The Message Translation excitingly puts Proverbs 18:20-21 this way:

> Words satisfy the mind as much as fruit does the stomach; good talk is as gratifying as a good harvest. Words kill; words give life; they're either poison or fruit—you choose.

Sticks and stones may break bones, but words can break the heart. Broken bones heal with time, but a crushed spirit is not easily repaired.

And James said:

It only takes a spark, remember, to set off a forest fire. A careless or wrongly placed word out of your mouth can do that. By our speech, we can ruin the world, turn harmony to chaos, throw mud on a reputation, send the whole world up in smoke and go up in smoke with it, smoke right from the pit of hell" (James 3:5-6MSG).

You may easily forget your words to others, but the recipients may nurture them over a lifetime. So make people feel happy, blessed, and motivated when they remember your words.

- Don't demotivate others.
- Don't discourage others

- Don't quench others' zeal

- Don't cause division or strife

- Don't peddle unfounded rumor

- Don't humiliate and embarrass others because they depend on you

- Don't make negative comparisons

- Don't put others down

- When angry, don't vent your anger with abusive, insulting words.

- Don't use swear and profane words when expressing displeasure

Blaise Pascal said, "Kind words do not cost much. Yet they accomplish much."

Your words are as powerful as your acts. Kindness in actions without kindness in words is incomplete.

Begin to sow the right word seeds. That's the foundation of profound life transformation.

Repeat after me:

"O Lord, empower my words henceforth to bring healing, encouragement, and peace. Teach me to plant the right word seeds every day, to be kind in words with people and in my relationships, in Jesus name."

Amen.

"If you don't like where you are now and what is happening, start your transformation by sowing the right Bible-based word seeds."

2

YOU WILL DECREE A THING; THAT IS, YOU, NOT SOMEONE ELSE

"Thou shalt also decree a thing, and it shall be established unto thee: and the light shall shine upon thy ways." - Job 22:28

Do you want light to shine on your way?

Then let's do what the Bible says to do.

Decree light.

It's not just up to God to cause light to shine in your way. God has done His part. The rest now lies in your hands.

But thank God, you know what to do.

Decree.

The scripture here didn't say, let's beg, cry, or get annoyed at life. It says thou shall decree a thing. It's definite.

STEP 1: YOU'RE THE ONE TO DECREE

You mean you. Not me, not your friend, not one prophet somewhere. You mean you. You are the one to decree something. Not another person.

Here's how it works: other people can pray for you, decree something for you, or project consequences for or against you. But none will be honored as much as the one you do for yourself. This means that no one can curse you without your consent. They may do that, but it will never happen if you don't accept it.

The same thing happens with the blessings people pronounce over you as well.

> *"People can say all kinds of blessings over you – that's good – but if you don't bless yourself, then their blessings will not happen."*

STEP 2: MAKE THE DECREE

I like what the dictionary says about the word decree. A decree is *an official order that has the force of law*.

Let me explain.

Many years ago, our country was ruled by the military. These military guys ruled by decrees, not by the constitution. This means that whatever they say is the law becomes the law. And that's what people have to follow. That's why they're called dictators.

Now, that's not a good system of governance because of the abuse, corruption, and power intoxication that goes with it. That's why the world prefers and recommends democracy – a type of government where the people decide how they should be governed.

Fortunately, or unfortunately, we don't operate by democracy in the spirit realm. We operate by decrees.

Physically, we run by the constitution. But spiritually, we work by decrees or orders.

Democracy is not practiced in the realm of the spirit. That's why you don't get justice simply because you deserve it. You get justice by enforcing it. You decree justice, and spiritual forces implement it.

Thankfully, our decrees are backed by God's law. Our decrees are official, and God works with them to create and recreate our world.

STEP 3: DECREE A THING

You shall decree something tangible, something real, and something you can see. It didn't say you shall think about a thing only. It says you shall decree A THING.

You can decree about your debt, about your health, about your children, about your career, or about your ministry.

Don't just worry about these things. Speak to them and pass decrees about them.

If you don't do that, the light will not shine on them. And no one will do it better for you.

I prayed with someone some time ago. While he was talking to me, the Holy Spirit said,

"Give him a spiritual assignment." I instructed him to wake up every midnight for seven days and begin to ***unsay*** every bad thing he had said about his life, business and health. He should conclude each session with communion to seal the new things he decreed.

Many of us need to be given that kind of assignment today. We need to go back and begin to unsay all the bad things we have been saying about ourselves, our health, finances, and our lives.

No one can help you if you believe you're doomed and that you're not coming out well in a situation. No one can change what you say about yourself because you are the most significant prophet of your life. Your thoughts and words create your circumstances.

Positive thinking is good, but without positive, prophetic words to order the contents of your thoughts, they are not created. Positive thinking must be backed by positive, prophetic speaking for the changes to happen.

In fact, you cannot think positively if you speak negatively. Your thinking and speaking must have tangible things they are focused on.

STEP 4: IT WILL BE ESTABLISHED

What you decree will be established. Other words for established are recognized, honored, proven, and done.

Here's how The Voice translation renders that verse:

> You will pronounce something to be, and He will make it so; light will break out across all of your paths.

So the word established there means that God will honor what you say.

It's interesting here because God also knows the bad things you say. If you constantly decree bad things, then darkness will break out across all your paths. But if what you decree are good things backed up by the Word, then light will break out across all your ways.

STEP 5: YOUR LIGHT WILL SHINE

Isn't that interesting? God created His light by saying, "Let there be light." You, too, can create the light of your life by decreeing it into existence. What you decree is what will be established, not what you wish, worry, and complain about.

There is power in your prophetic words. Now let's use that power and change everything that needs to changed.

> *"...No one can curse you without your consent. They may do that, but if you don't accept it, then it will never happen."*

3

THE DIFFERENCE BETWEEN POSITIVE CONFESSION AND PROPHETIC DECLARATION

---

8 But what saith it? The word is nigh thee, even in thy mouth, and in thy heart: that is, the word of faith, which we preach;

9 That if thou shalt confess with thy mouth the Lord Jesus, and shalt believe in thine heart that God hath raised him from the dead, thou shalt be saved. 10 For with the heart man believeth unto righteousness, and with the mouth, confession is made unto salvation–
Rom. 10: 8-10

Note this scripture carefully. We will come back to it in a few minutes. For now, let's answer the question, *what's the difference between positive confession and prophetic declaration?*

A prophetic declaration is different from a positive confession. If you don't understand this, you may think they are the same. But they are not.

Positive confession is just saying nice, pleasant, good things about yourself...

- I'm alright
- I'm living a good life
- My life is in good shape
- I feel excellent
- I will succeed, and so on

While there is nothing wrong with that, in fact, talking like that is okay, but prophetic declaration is different.

Prophetic declaration is declaring the word of God. You find scriptures regarding something and continuously declare it. That way, you send that scripture on a mission. You release it to angels to bring it to pass.

For instance, instead of only saying some beautiful things, you say Biblical positions about your life. You turn those beautiful statements into spiritual bullets by empowering them with scripture.

- I am healed by the stripes of Jesus (Isa53:4-5)

- I walk in good health even as my soul prospers (3John 1:2).

- God will satisfy me with a long, healthy life and save me at the end (Psalm 91:16)

- As the days of a tree, so will my days be (Isaiah 65:20)

- God provides all my *needs* according to his riches, so I lack nothing (Phil. 4:19).

- Everything is working out for my good (Romans 8:28)

- The hearts of everyone is working for my favor (Proverbs 21:1)

- The Lord is my shepherd, so I do not lack anything (Psalm 23:1)

- My going out will be a blessing, and my coming back will be a blessing (Deut. 28:6, Psalm 121:8)

- Whatever I lay my hands will prosper (Psalm 1:1-3)

- My wife shall be a fruitful vine and my children like olive shoots round about my table (Psalm 128:1-3)

- I shall be a lender, not a borrower

- I am dwelling in God's presence all the days of my life (Psalm 91:1)

- God is with me everywhere I go; I will not be afraid (Isaiah 41:10, Matt. 28:20)

- When I go through rivers or fire, they will not swallow or burn me because God is with me (Isaiah 43:2)

- No man born of woman has the power to hurt me (Luke 12:4).

Do you see the difference?

In positive confessions, you say kind and pleasant things about yourself, but in prophetic declaration, you **say scripture things** about yourself. You take scriptures and declare them; that way, you commit God's integrity to make them come to pass.

It's okay to master positive confessions, but it's far better and more life-changing to learn prophetic confessions. You say them so much until they become your daily confessions.

Now, look at our opening scripture. It says:

> 8 But what saith it? The word is nigh thee, even in thy mouth, and in thy heart: that is, the word of faith, which we preach;

> 9 That if thou shalt confess with thy mouth the Lord Jesus, and shalt believe in thine heart that God hath raised him from the dead, thou shalt be saved. 10 For with the heart man believeth unto righteousness, and with the mouth, confession is made unto salvation.

There are two implications of this scripture. First, to be saved from sin and become heaven-bound, born again Christian, one must believe with their heart that God raised Jesus from the dead. Then one must confess Jesus Christ as their Lord and Savior. That's what the scripture is saying. But there's more.

We know that Jesus is the WORD. So to confess with thy mouth the Lord Jesus also means to declare the WORD of God. When you declare the Word and believe in your heart what you declare, you commit the Holy Spirit to bring you salvation in that area.

Confessing the Word of God about your health, finances, family, or career is the same as admitting that Jesus is Lord over your health, He is Lord over your finances, He is Lord over your family, He is Lord over your career, and so on.

Why is understanding the difference between positive confession and prophetic confession very important? Simple. Because the Holy Spirit works with the Word of God and quickens it to come to pass. He does not work with the words of the flesh.

So, you want God to be committed to bringing to pass what you say? Then declare His word, not yours. That's the difference between prophetic declaration and positive confession.

SPEAK BY HIS INSPIRATION

There is another part of prophetic confession I need to bring to your attention. Psalm 81:10 captures it this way:

"I am the Lord thy God, which brought thee out of the land of Egypt: open thy mouth wide, and I will fill it."

Here, you open your mouth and declare as the Lord inspires your heart. You come in the place of prayer, worship, study, or you're simply walking home, and you begin to declare specific words of healing, deliverance, protection, promotion, favor, or whatever, as inspired by the Holy Spirit in your heart. It's not the same with ordinary positive confession because you are passing decrees based on utterances imparted by the Holy Spirit. And God is committed to making these declarations stand.

Sometimes you start from the physical and then follow the inspiration of the Holy Spirit as He gives you utterance of what to say. You can begin like…

> "This is the day the Lord has made. I will rejoice and be glad in it.
>
> "Today, favor will speak for me everywhere I go. I have favor with my boss and with everyone in the office.
>
> "I am a blessing to my generation.
>
> "My children will call me blessed. They will grow in the knowledge and power of God…"

As you continue declaring, suddenly, great inspirational thoughts start flowing into your heart. Then you begin to release them from your mouth. Without pre-planning, you could suddenly burst out saying mysterious things…

- No, no, no. There shall be no death. I shall not die.

- This ministry will succeed. We have 200 new souls this year, in the name of Jesus Christ.

- I say no to the angels of death against my mother.

- Jayson, you will come to the Lord Jesus Christ. You will be saved.

- You demons of cancer, loose your grips on Isabella today.

And on and on, you decree as the utterance flows.

HOLD FAST THE CONFESSION

Let us hold fast the confession of our hope without wavering, for He who promised is faithful. – Hebrews 10:23

Having discovered what the confession of faith, confession of hope, prophetic confession, or prophetic declaration means, let us hold fast to it. Why? Because He who promised us is faithful.

The promises will work out as declared and confessed. We may not be seeing it now, but they will undoubtedly come to pass.

The term *hold fast* means to be tenacious with the word, persistent with our confessions, and resist any thought, idea, or attack against it. Your prophetic declarations will come to pass because God's word is Yeah and Amen.

"You want God to be committed to bringing to pass what you say? Then declare His word, not yours. That's the difference between prophetic declaration and positive confession."

4

BY THIS TIME TOMORROW

Elisha replied, "The Lord says that by this time tomorrow, two gallons of flour or four gallons of barley grain will be sold in the markets of Samaria for a dollar!" – 2Kings 7:1 (TLB)

Before we get into this particular verse, here's a background of what happened. The Assyrian king, Benhadad, warred with Israel. He and his army besieged Samaria, the capital of Israel, and prevented people, goods, and services from going in and out of the city. As a result, there was a massive famine in Israel.

The hunger (or you could say *economic recession*) was so bad that a pint of dove's shit sold for three dollars.

> Later on, however, King Ben-hadad of Syria mustered his entire army and besieged Samaria. 25 As a result, there was a great famine in the city, and after a long while, even a donkey's head sold for fifty dollars, and a pint of dove's dung brought three dollars! – 2Kings 6:24-25 (TLB)

That wasn't all. Things got severer to the extent that some families started killing their children to eat.

> One day as the king of Israel was walking along the city wall, a woman called to him, "Help, my lord, the king!""If the Lord doesn't help you, what can I do?" he retorted. "I have neither food nor wine to give you. However, what's the matter?"
>
> She replied, "This woman proposed that we eat my son one day and her son the next. So we

boiled my son and ate him, but the next day when I said, 'Kill your son so we can eat him,' she hid him." – 2 Kings 6: 26-30

This was the height of the suffering. On hearing that women had started eating their children, the king was provoked to the extent he decided to do something about it. He decided to talk to Prophet Elisha, and if Elisha did not help the situation, he would kill him.

But what was the offense of Elisha here? He didn't bring the famine on the land. Israel's sins forced God's anger on them, and now they were suffering. Why blame Elisha?

This is the way of the world. They always find ways to blame God's prophets for bad things in the land as if they were the ones that caused it to happen. In Africa, for example, people say something like, "why are you building a cathedral when there are no good schools in the country?" Then when a church builds schools, they say, "Why are you spending all that money to build schools when people are hungry? Don't you see so many poor people around?" They blame preachers for the failure of the government.

I agree that there are areas to hold preachers responsible, but you don't go blaming them for the failure of the government to provide jobs, plan the economy, and create a sound health care system.

How often do we create problems for ourselves and then blame God? That's what the king of Israel did. He sent men to Elisha with the words, "I will kill you today if you don't stop this famine."

Faithful ministers of God are the spiritual gatekeepers of their nations; they hold access to the spiritual destiny of the land. In a time of crisis, kings are expected to reach out to them for help. When and if they pray, the nation's destiny is released from the hands of the enemy.

I believe that Elisha has been interceding for the nation over the famine. So, when the king's message came to him, even though the intentions and plans for the man of God were evil, he had a word from the Lord. By the inspiration of the Holy Spirit, he said,

> "By this time tomorrow, two gallons of flour or four gallons of barley grain will be sold in the markets of Samaria for a dollar!"

That was unheard of, judging by the situation on the ground. Which production strategy will generate such capacity in twenty-four hours?

It was evident that this was faith taken too far.

But the prophet had spoken.

Unfortunately, instead of the king's messenger to agree and say amen, he analyzed the situation and replied, "Mr. Prophet," he said, "This is not possible. Even if God opens the sky and lets food items out, this can't happen."

Look at that! You came to the man of God for help. He speaks by inspiration and says this is what will happen; instead of agreeing with what he said, you start telling him, "It's not possible. This kind of thing has never happened before."

If you visualize the mindset of this officer well, you'll see a man mocking the prophet and his declaration. You'll see a man telling the prophet that he was out of his mind even to suggest a thing like that could happen.

Unfortunately, he failed to realize that God does not operate on human laws. He didn't know that:

> *"Divinely inspired prophetic declaration sets off some spiritual protocols that upturn physical conditions and command impossible situations to become possible."*

The prophet replied to him, "Sir, you will see it, but you will not partake of it."

"Really!" he must have thought. And because he didn't believe the prophet in the first place, he didn't bother to say, "I'm sorry. Plead for mercy for me." He was like, "Let's see how it goes?"

What happened?

Right from when the prophetic word was released, a series of events started to unfold. The next day, everything happened precisely as Elisha declared. Unfortunately, the man who doubted the prophetic word saw it but did not partake of it.

> [18] You recall that this man of God had told the king, "By this time tomorrow, 7 quarts of premium flour will sell for 11 grams, and 13 quarts of barley will sell for the same at the market in the gate of Samaria." [19] The officer had then asked, "Even if the Eternal carved out windows in heaven, is it possible?" Elisha had replied, "You will witness this event, but you will not be allowed to enjoy the feast." [20] This was the truth about the officer's destiny, for he was killed at the city entrance—trampled by the starving, miserable citizens of Samaria. – 2Kings 7:18-20

Okay, that's the story. But what are the lessons?

GOD'S WAYS CANNOT BE UNDERSTOOD OR EXPLAINED

No law on earth could have made the prophetic word Elisha gave to happen. No scientific theory, research, or discovery could have explained that. That was why the king's messenger wondered what Elisha took to make him say something like that. Only God's supernatural working can make a nation with no food for many months to have a surplus the following day.

When you make prophetic declarations, don't bother about the logical and technical reality on the ground. Don't mind the details of how the healing will happen and how the situation will change. Just continue to decree as you are led. The situation will change. Yours is to decree and declare, and let God's power work out the decrees you give.

DON'T BE AFRAID TO DECREE

Your prophetic declarations start the spiritual procedures that upturn the physical situations and bring about a change. But you must stand and make the decrees, and sometimes you must continue making the decrees without recourse to the physical condition of things at the moment.

In this story, one thing to remember is that it was not easy for Elisha to say what he said. It's one thing for God to say, *this is what will happen.* But it's another thing for someone to have the boldness to repeat that revelation or inspiration before people. I'm sure Elisha called himself a crazy man after that prophetic declaration.

But I've come to learn that sometimes we don't have to make sense to make news. Declare the word, in season and out of season, when it makes sense and when it doesn't make sense. You don't have to be understood by everyone. Let them misunderstand you at the beginning so that when you stand, they will understand.

> *"Say what God is saying about your health, about your marriage, about your family, about your finances, and about your tomorrow. Say it privately and say it publicly when you can. Say it on social media and everywhere you can. Don't be afraid to make the declarations. They will undoubtedly come to pass."*

When we come to church on Sundays, we get bombarded with the fire of God's Word. We jump and shout and sing and tumble up and down in ecstasy. Unfortunately, the moment we leave the church, everything dies down. We forget everything and go back to asking, "O Lord, what have I done?"

That's the wrong way to treat the word you hear. Don't let the fire end on Sunday. Take it home and use it to light up everything around you for the rest of the week.

When reality comes looking at you on Sunday evening or Monday morning, start shouting back at it. Remind it that God only rested but didn't stop working. Rise and boldly declare prophetically over the situation and never back down. Your prophetic words will change your life.

WITH GOD, NOTHING IS IMPOSSIBLE

As I meditated over this story, I imagined that if this were Jesus, Peter would have accosted him after the prophecy and said, "Sir, did you hear yourself? Are you sure this is not overboard? I think we need to be a bit more careful with these guys."

And Jesus would have gently replied to him and the other apostles, "With man, this is impossible, but not with God; all things are possible with God."

To be honest, if I were there, I would have encouraged my master, Elisha, to be a little bit more diplomatic. Imagine that he asked me to go and tell that messenger that *by this time tomorrow, there would be so much food in the land that things would be too cheap.* I would have gone to the man, and this is probably what I would have done.

The messenger: "What did your master, the prophet, say?"

Me: "You know sir, emm, emmm…yes…you know, actually, you see, the prophet said I should let you know that he's praying and that God will do something soon."

But that's not what God said. That's not what the prophet said.

Thank God that today, as I read and think about it, I see my weakness and unbelief, and I can ask God for mercy.

We must pray that God will help our unbelief.

May His mercy speak for us where our unbelief has spoken against His power and grace in the past, in Jesus name.

Amen.

Do yourself a favor and stop wondering how the scriptures you speak and the words you declare by the Holy Spirit would come to pass.

That part is not your job. Do yours and let God worry about His part.

Our human mind can never comprehend the depth of God, His power, and the mystery of His grace. So yes, the doctor may say, "honey, this is bad." But you go home and say, "Not really. In the name of Jesus Christ, I'm walking in divine health."

How will it happen? You don't know, but you'll say and keep saying what God is saying.

People around may think you're getting out of your mind and feel you need some help, but that's their business. They're entitled to their side of the story. For you, this is what God's word says, and that's what you are saying.

The pregnancy test result comes back negative, and this is after ten years. You say, "Well, I know that I am like an olive shoot. My children and I will surround my husband's table. I cannot be barren."

You go home, and your concerned friends say, "Dear, you'll be forty-seven tomorrow, and you'll be embracing menopause already." You look at them and say, "I cannot be barren. I will bear children."

Faith doesn't always make sense. But keep speaking the word. Say what God is saying even when it doesn't make sense. For with God, nothing shall be impossible. He does not operate with human laws.

SPEAK THE INSPIRED WORD, DON'T WAIT FOR VALIDATION

Another takeaway from this story is that when God puts words of inspiration in your heart about your life, health, family, and future, speak. Don't consult. Don't look for validation.

Imagine if Elisha sat down and began to reason with Gehazi, his servant, or reason with other prophets. They would have told him to hold on for a moment. And they would have found a hundred reasons for him to delay the prophecy. One smart elder-prophet there would have said, "Since God said tomorrow food would be abundant, let's relax. When it happens tomorrow, they will see it, and we would tell them that's what God said."

And the council of elders there would have nodded in agreement. That way, they would presume to save the man of God from embarrassment if nothing happens tomorrow. And if it happens, they would also say, "Yeah! We threaded carefully."

Unfortunately, God doesn't work that way. You don't wait for the miracle to happen before you declare the word God puts in your heart. You declare it for the miracle to happen.

If Elisha had not proclaimed the prophetic word, the miracle would not have happened. The suffering would have continued if he had followed some common sense, diplomatic method to appear friendly.

> *"If you don't declare the word, the miracle will not happen."*

You don't wait to see the healing manifest before you say, *"I am healed by the stripes of Jesus Christ. I am walking in divine health."* You say it and keep saying it to see the miracle.

You don't wait for the money to be in your account before you say, *"I am rich. I have enough. I am a lender, not a borrower. I am lending to nations. I have all that I need."*

You say it and continue saying it before you're empowered to see it.

If you're waiting for the doctor's final report before you say you're healed, you're not walking by faith, and you're not speaking your healing into existence. Let the doctors do their job, but you'll not stop saying what God has said, the physical symptoms notwithstanding.

Speak the word. Don't wait for validation. Don't wait for approval, and don't wait for the weather to show promising signs first. Your prophetic words are what changes the situation.

"Faith doesn't always make sense. But keep speaking the word. Say what God is saying even when it doesn't make sense. For with God, nothing shall be impossible. He does not operate with human laws."

5

SPEAK TO THE MOUNTAIN, NOT ABOUT IT

₂₂So Jesus answered and said to them, "Have faith in God. ₂₃For assuredly, I say to you, whoever says to this mountain, 'Be removed and be cast into the sea,' and does not doubt in his heart, but believes that those things he says will be done, he will have whatever he says. ₂₄Therefore, I say to you, whatever things you ask when you pray, believe that you receive them, and you will have them. – Mark 11:22-24

This story is one of the most powerful lessons Jesus taught His disciples on faith. The previous day, he had approached a fig tree expecting to find fruits in it. Unfortunately, the tree didn't have any fruits. He spoke to it and said, *"You shall never bear fruit again!"* And the disciples heard him say it.

So, on this very day, as they passed the same place, the disciples saw that the fig tree had died and remembered that Jesus had cursed the tree the previous day. Excitedly, they came to Jesus and said, ***"Master, look at that tree that you cursed. It's dead."*** Obviously, they didn't expect that the fig tree would die so quickly or that it would die at all.

Then Jesus replied and said that if they had faith, they could speak to any mountain, and it would move out of its place and go elsewhere and that whatever they asked for in payer, they would receive.

What are the core lessons for us in this story?

1. Jesus spoke to the fig tree, the mountain, not about it. He didn't start analyzing the tree and how it should have or not have fruit. He simply said, *"May no man eat fruit from you, henceforth."*

If there is a mountain standing before you right now, a mountain that needs to be moved, speak to it. Don't start analyzing it. Leave the analyses to the experts. Just get into your room and start speaking to it:

- "You debt, in the name of Jesus Christ, move. Cease."

- "You marine spirit that appears to me in the dream, leave now. My body is the temple of the Holy Spirit."

- "These gatherings and meetings against the ministry…, scatter in the name of Jesus Christ."

Speak to the mountain. That's what Jesus said you should do, not analyze the situation.

2. Faith speaks to the situation and not about the situation. You don't have to analyze the situation. Just speak to it and leave the details. Talking about the condition or explaining it breeds doubt and fear and gets you out of faith.

3. Jesus didn't care about the immediate outcome. He didn't also hide while speaking to the tree. The disciples may have thought, *"Okay, let's see what will happen."* And when the tree didn't die immediately, they may have thought again, *"Hmmm! This one didn't work."*

But as long as Jesus was concerned, what others thought and said was irrelevant. He spoke to the tree and moved on.

4. Think less of what people will say. If you're going to walk in faith, then you're going to bother less about what people will think and say. Only act according to the revealed word in your heart and move on. Leave the analyzing and talking to the observers and followers.

5. Sometimes, your actions and words of faith will not produce immediate results. But that doesn't mean they're not working. The fig tree did not die immediately. But it died eventually.

You may not be seeing the results of your faith actions and speaking now, but they are working. Keep speaking to the mountains of your life; they will certainly leave.

Make these declarations before we proceed:

> Today, Lord, I chose to speak to everything that represents mountains in my life. I refuse to analyze and get angry over the things that need to change in my life and family henceforth.
>
> I chose to move every mountain from this moment by faith. And I am confident that my

faith actions and words will work out the purpose of God for my life. I will not be moved when I don't see instant results, for I am confident that God's Word never fails.

I now command all mountains and obstacles before me to disappear this day.

> *"Recognize your mountains and begin to speak to them in the name of Jesus Christ. That's the way to move them."*

THE GOD KIND OF FAITH

When God began creating the earth, it was a mass of nothingness, a shapeless, chaotic, bottomless emptiness. The Bible says that darkness covered everywhere. Then God began to speak. Genesis 1 says:

- [3] Then God said, "Let there be light," and there was light.

- ₆ Then God said, "Let there be a firmament in the midst of the waters, and let it divide the waters from the waters." And it was so.

- ₉ Then God said, "Let the waters under the heavens be gathered together into one place and let the dry land appear," and it was so. ...

As God spoke, light came. As He spoke, things took shape. As He spoke, order came.

By the word of the Lord, the heavens were made, and all the host of them by the breath of His mouth - Psalm 33:6

God created the world by speaking into existence the things in His heart. He spoke the results, and the chaotic present gave way.

God's kind of faith is a speaking faith. He spoke His intentions, and they came to pass.

When Jesus spoke to the fig tree, He was doing what He had seen the Father do (John 5:19). He was speaking God's Word and believing it to be fulfilled just as He desired it to happen.

> *"We are imitators of Christ, called to do what we see Jesus doing and to say what we hear Him saying. We have to release our faith through our words."*

Faith talks. Faith is not to keep silent and hope that things will change. No. You have to speak, speak, speak, and speak. Follow God's example by proclaiming what your results will be.

If you need healing, you can boldly say, "I am healed" because Isaiah 53:5 promises that Jesus paid the price for your healing.

If you need a job or provision, you can declare, according to Philippians 4:19, that God meets your every need according to His riches in Christ Jesus.

If you need peace, you can thank God for His peace that passes understanding that guards your heart and mind even in a troubled world (Philippians 4:7).

Create your world and experiences by the words of faith you declare every day. The God kind of faith is a speaking faith. Now say after me:

> *I have the God kind of faith. I am created in the image of God. I am an imitator of Christ. As God created the world through His Words, I am creating and re-creating my world, the events of my life, and experiences with my words aligned to God's word.*
>
> *As I decree things in line with the Word, I see them happen. I will not be discouraged by the past. I know who I am now and will never give up to defeat or failure anymore, in Jesus name.*

Amen.

"Faith talks. Faith is not to keep silent and hope that things will change. No. You have to speak, speak, speak, and speak."

6

SPEAK TO THE STORM; DON'T LET IT SPEAK TO YOU

If there is a storm in your life right now, arise and shout to it in the name of Jesus Christ. And keep shouting at it until there is calm.

Here's a fascinating story of what happened in the Bible. The same problem for everyone in the boat, but different responses.

I love the way The Voice version of the Bible renders the story. I love the dramatization in it and how it smoothly flows. Please read this story as we proceed:

35 The same evening, Jesus suggested they cross over to the other side of the lake. 36 With Jesus already in the boat, they left the crowd behind and set sail along with a few other boats that followed. 37 As they sailed, a storm formed. The winds whipped up huge waves that broke over the bow, filling the boat with so much water that even the experienced sailors among them were sure they were going to sink.

38 Jesus was back in the stern of the boat, sound asleep on a cushion when the disciples shook Him awake.

Disciples (shouting over the storm): Jesus, Master, don't You care that we're going to die?

39 He got up, shouted words into the wind, and commanded the waves.

Jesus: "That's enough! Be still!" And immediately the wind died down to nothing, the waves stopped.

Jesus: 40 How can you be so afraid? After all, you've seen, where is your faith?

In my daily audio broadcast, I took three days to teach from this scripture. I felt the presence of God as I spoke from it. I felt the Holy Spirit nudging in my heart, saying, "That's what is important. That's what I want my people to do."

From this story, we see compelling lessons for supernatural manifestation.

1. EVERYONE FACES A STORM

As I studied this scripture, the first thing that came to my mind was, "Jesus was in their boat, yet a storm attacked them. I thought that with Jesus in there, the storm was barred from attacking. How is that?"

The lesson is that everyone, believer or no believer, will face storms at some point in their lives. Being a Christian does not shield us from the storm. There will always come a time that the wind blows against everyone. Some have gone through harsh storms in life, some are going through some storms presently, and some will go through storms in the future. However, some will be powerfully defined badly by their storms, while some will be mightily made by their storms.

Everyone faces a storm, but we don't all get the same endings, outcomes, and results. Only those who invest their lives in the Word of God are guaranteed to survive any storm. Instead of the storms destroying them, the storms move them to their destinies.

So relax, the storms may come, but they will not destroy you. Through the Holy Spirit, you will be empowered to overcome every storm that comes your way at any point in your life.

Don't feel bad if there is a situation in your life that currently looks like a storm. It will not consume you. You will come out of it stronger and better. Jesus is with you, so the storm will not devour you no matter how fierce it appears.

2. THE TARGET OF THE STORM IS TO STOP THE PURPOSE OF GOD

Why did the storm attack the boat? Was it because it wanted to destroy Jesus and His disciples? My answer is no. The storm's attention was on the purpose of God, not on the persons in the boat.

> *"When the devil senses a divine purpose, he doesn't mind destroying a whole nation, just to stop that purpose."*

Remember how Herod killed all male kids from two years down just because he wanted to kill Christ. A Pharaoh killed all male children to stop the Israelites from multiplying according to divine purpose.

Check thoroughly whenever the devil attacks; he is after God's purpose, not the persons involved.

Jesus had told the disciples, "Let's go over to the other side." When you see what happened on the other side, you'll understand why this movement was very strategic and why the devil wanted to stop it at all costs.

On the other side, many miracles took place. The sick were healed, those possessed by demons were delivered, and God's kingdom expanded. But one of the deliverance cases is very noteworthy.

The moment the boat landed successfully, a man possessed by thousands of demons ran to Jesus for help.

₂ And when He had come out of the boat, immediately there met Him out of the tombs a man with an unclean spirit, ₃ who had his dwelling among the tombs; and no one could bind him, not even with chains, ₄ because he had often been bound with shackles and chains. And the chains had been pulled apart by him, and the shackles broken in pieces; neither could anyone tame him. ₅ And always, night and day, he was in the mountains and in the tombs, crying out and cutting himself with stones. – Mark 5:2-5

Imagine how this man suffered in the hands of demons. They made him a mockery in the community and almost destroyed him.

No wonder the devil didn't want Jesus coming over to that side! He had seen that if Jesus came to that town, their prey would be delivered, and the man would become a great asset to the Kingdom of God. So, he sent a storm to stop Jesus from coming.

But to the glory of God, the storm failed.

⁶ When he saw Jesus from afar, he ran and worshipped Him. ⁷ And he cried out with a loud voice and said, "What have I to do with You, Jesus, Son of the Most High God? I implore You by God that You do not torment me."

⁸ For He said to him, "Come out of the man, unclean spirit!" ⁹ Then He asked him, **"What is your name?"** And he answered, saying, "My name is Legion; for we are many." ¹⁰ Also, he begged Him earnestly that He would not send them out of the country.

¹¹ Now, a large herd of swine was feeding there near the mountains. ¹² So all the demons begged Him, saying, "Send us to the swine, that we may enter them." ¹³ And at once Jesus gave them permission. Then the unclean spirits went out and entered the swine (there were about two thousand), and the herd ran violently down the steep place into the sea and drowned in the sea.

¹⁸ And when He got into the boat, he who had been demon-possessed begged Him that he

might be with Him. ₁₉ However, Jesus did not permit him, but said to him, **"Go home to your friends, and tell them what great things the Lord has done for you, and how He has had compassion on you."** ₂₀ *And he departed and began to proclaim in Decapolis all that Jesus had done for him, and all marveled. – Mark 5: 6-18*

This delivered man became an instant evangelist, sharing what God did in his town and the neighboring cities.

What if Jesus had not reached this place because of the storm? What if He had said, *"Let's turn back and sail on a different day?"* This man would not have been delivered, and he would not have shared the good news in those places.

The lesson here is that the motivation of the devil in every storm is to stop the purpose of God. When he sends a storm, you're not the target; God's purpose for your life is what the target is.

When you know this, you will begin to see the big picture in every storm in your life. You will start to see why you must not succumb to the storm and why you must do what Jesus did to the storm and never allow yourself to be destroyed.

If there is a storm in your life or family now, it will fail. Don't let it stop you from the big picture – God's purpose for your life.

3. DON'T LOSE YOUR PEACE IN THE STORM

The first and most important thing you need in any storm is peace. Without peace and calmness, you will negatively react to the storm. You will not discern what is happening in the spirit, and you will miss the purpose of God.

As I meditated on this scripture, one question that didn't stop popping up in my heart was, "How was Jesus able to sleep in such a situation?"

Imagine the confusion in the boat. Imagine the sailors struggling fruitlessly to keep the ship afloat. Imagine the disciples (passengers) running up and down and shouting everywhere. Yet Jesus was sleeping. How did he manage to do that?

Jesus maintained such an enormous amount of peace for two reasons:

(i). He deliberately shut himself off from the chaotic atmosphere of fear and confusion: When the disciples were shouting up and down, running helter-skelter, was Jesus so deep in sleep that he didn't notice the mess? What really happened?

The truth is that it would take someone excessively stressed or suffering from a health condition to be in such a deep sleep. I believe Jesus knew what was happening but refused to let the fear and pandemonium get into his spirit. He deliberately built a mental wall against the raging atmosphere.

To keep your peace in the storm, you must deliberately refuse to yield to the fear, confusion, and mayhem that the storm is trying to transfer. Sometimes this may mean staying away from the negative news; sometimes, it may mean shutting yourself from social media; and sometimes, it may mean refusing to get involved in any discussion that glorifies the problem.

Whatever you can, try to keep yourself away from everything that increases your fear and doubt. Fear is usually more dangerous than any danger. Jesus knew about the danger of letting himself join in the uproar, so he shut himself off from the chaos by sleeping.

When there is a storm in your life, deliberately refuse to yield your spirit to fear and worry.

> *"Shut off anything that feeds your confusion and feed more on God's word."*

You need peace to connect and draw from the wells of salvation.

(ii). Jesus was conscious of the presence of God: A consciousness of God's presence is a powerful secret for maintaining peace in a storm. Jesus was relaxed in the storm because he had that unbeatable consciousness.

The same way that God was with Jesus on earth is the same way He is with you today. You may not feel it, but He is with you. Things may be ugly, but He is with you. The storm may look very fierce right now, but God is with you. You may feel your prayers are not getting answered, but God is with you. You must have this assurance, no matter what happens. That's the key to having peace in a storm.

Come to terms with this reality: God is with you, even if you are passing through the valley of the shadow of death. He is with you even if you are passing through the rivers or through the fire. Even when it seems you are critically ill, God is with you.

When you are surrounded by enemies, God is with you. They will not destroy you. Remind yourself uncompromisingly about that whenever there is any storm in your life. Keep saying and declaring: *"God is with me. I may not feel, but I know it."*

They that are with you are greater than they that are with them. Compose a song about the presence of God and make it your prayer and discussions.

When the army of Syria surrounded Elisha, Elisha had no reason to fear. Initially troubled, his servant asked, *"Oh no, my lord! What shall we do?"* The prophet replied and said, "Don't be afraid, those who are with us are more than those who are with them" (2 Kings 6:14-17).

Then Elisha prayed, "Open his eyes, Lord, so that he may see." Then the Lord opened the servant's eyes, and he looked and saw the hills full of horses and chariots of fire all around Elisha.

If you pray the same prayer, God will show you. You can pray from your heart and say, "Lord, I am afraid in this storm. Your word says that you are with me. Please assure me of Your presence."

God will, in some way, show forth and assure your heart of His presence. Whether you see a vision or not is irrelevant. God is with you, and He will prove it.

However, believe even without seeing any signs. For "blessed are those who have not seen and yet have believed."

> ***Don't wait for signs to believe.***
> ***Take God at His word.***

He said:

Joshua 1:9 – "Have I not commanded you? Be strong and courageous. Do not be afraid; do not be discouraged, for the Lord your God will be with you wherever you go."

Isaiah 41:10 – "So do not fear, for I am with you; do not be dismayed, for I am your God. I will strengthen you and help you; I will uphold you with my righteous right hand.

3. DON'T BE AFRAID; SPEAK TO THE STORM

Did you notice what Jesus asked them after the storm had calmed? He said to them, "How can you be so afraid? After all you've seen, where is your faith?"

In other words, the storm would have calmed if the disciples had stood up and spoken to it in faith without waking Jesus. That's what Jesus meant. He was simply telling them,

> "You could have spoken to the storm and calmed it. You don't need to be afraid. I am with you. You've seen a lot of miracles. By now, you should have known that with God, nothing is impossible, and as long as I am

here, the storm will not destroy you. So why don't you put your faith to work?"

This is the same thing Jesus is telling you today. He is with you, so the storm will never destroy you. Continue to speak peace to any storm in your life right now. The power is with you – in your mouth.

"When there is a storm in your life, deliberately refuse to yield your spirit to fear and worry. Shut off anything that feeds your confusion, and feed more on God's word. You need peace to connect and draw from the wells of salvation."

7

DON'T BURY THE CHILD YET

Children are gifts from God. They light up the home and bring happiness to everyone. They are treasures that keep us strong and going when there is no reason to keep hope alive. When they are hurt, we are hurt. When they are in pain, we are in pain. If they die, we feel lost.

Your children will not die, in Jesus name.

Amen.

But this chapter is not entirely about children. It's about the things that light up your life, your hope, the things that mean a lot to your destiny, your visions, your ideas, your prayer expectations, and so on. I call them your child(ren), and I am telling you by the Holy Spirit today, don't bury them yet.

Does it look like they are dying or dead already? God says, "Don't bury them yet."

The Bible tells us an exciting story about a woman whose child died. What she did was amazing. She refused to bury the child, and God brought her boy back to life. Let's read this story to see what happened and learn from what she did.

> 18 When the child was grown, the day came that he went out to his father, to the reapers. 19 But he said to his father, "My head, my head." The man said to his servant, "Carry him to his mother."
>
> 20 When he had carried and brought him to his mother, he sat on her lap until noon, and then he died. 21 She went up and laid him on the bed of the man of God and shut the door [of the small upper room] behind him and left.

22 Then she called to her husband and said, "Please send me one of the servants and one of the donkeys, so that I may run to the man of God and return." 23 He said, "Why are you going to him today? It is neither the New Moon nor the Sabbath." And she said, "It will be all right." 24 Then, she saddled the donkey and said to her servant, "Drive [the animal] fast; do not slow down the pace for me unless I tell you." 25 So she set out and came to the man of God at Mount Carmel.

When the man of God saw her at a distance, he said to Gehazi, his servant, "Look, there is the Shunammite woman. 26 Please run now to meet her and ask her, 'Is it well with you? Is it well with your husband? Is it well with the child?'" And she answered, "It is well."

27 When she came to the mountain to the man of God, she took hold of his feet. Gehazi approached to push her away, but the man of God said, "Let her alone, for her soul is desperate and troubled within her; and the Lord has hidden the reason from me and has not told

me." 28 Then she said, "Did I ask for a son from my lord? Did I not say, 'Do not give me false hope'?"

29 Then he said to Gehazi, "Gird up your loins (prepare now!) and take my staff in your hand, and go [to the woman's house]; if you meet any man [along the way], do not greet him and if a man greets you, do not [stop to] answer him; and lay my staff on the face of the boy [as soon as you reach the house]."

30 The mother of the child said, "As the Lord lives and as your soul lives, I will not leave you." So Elisha arose and followed her.

31 Gehazi went on ahead of them and laid the staff on the boy's face, but there was no sound or response [from the boy]. So he turned back to meet Elisha and told him, "The boy has not awakened (revived)."

32 When Elisha came into the house, the child was dead and lying on his bed. 33 So he went in, shut the door behind the two of them, and prayed to the Lord.

₃₄ Then he went up and lay on the child and put his mouth on his mouth, his eyes on his eyes, and his hands on his hands. And as he stretched himself out on him and held him, the boy's skin became warm.

₃₅ Then he returned and walked in the house once back and forth, and went up again and stretched himself out on him; and the boy sneezed seven times and he opened his eyes.

₃₆ Then Elisha called Gehazi and said, "Call this Shunammite." So he called her. And when she came to him, he said, "Pick up your son." ₃₇ She came and fell at his feet, bowing herself to the ground in respect and gratitude. Then she picked up her son and left. – 2 Kings 4:18-37 (AMP)

Do you see what I see here? This story demonstrates that anything is possible if we believe and refuse to give up. The Holy Spirit brought a few thoughts to my spirit as I read and thought through this story.

MIRACLES ARE NOT FINAL

Does God's gift get sick?

To appreciate the reason for this question, you must understand the circumstances behind the birth of the boy in this story. He was a special gift from God to the family, an answer to Prophet Elisha's prayer.

If this boy was born after prayers, why did he get sick and even die? I thought that because He was a miracle child from God, he should have lived in perfect health all his life.

Well, you have to understand that miracles are not final. That is why it is perilous to stop going to church, stop giving, stop praying, and stop serving just because you received your miracle. You will never come to a point in your life where you won't need God.

> **"The world we live in lies in awful darkness. The devil never gives up. He keeps trying to attack to dampen our faith."**

That's why someone can receive healing after prayers and get sick later. That's why someone can get delivered from a stronghold and be attacked with something else later.

Think about this: you prayed, and God sent your husband. Praise God. But that's not the end of the story. That's not the end of your need for prayers and God's help. You will need to build a family and raise children. And that will require daily faith, wisdom, and support from God.

When I see people who quit church, stopped serving, and let their zeal grow cold just because they got a job, a business, a contract, or made some money, I wonder the ignorance.

This *"I have arrived mentality"* is the easiest way to knock oneself out of God's bigger picture and open the door for the devil in one's life.

Let this story instruct you against this type of life. This boy was a gift from God, but the devil attacked later. But thank God the receiver was still in the spiritual position to seek divine restoration. And that's the point. We must continually be in the spiritual attitude to stand against the devil's attack when it comes.

IF YOUR FAITH SAYS YES, GOD WILL NOT SAY NO

One area that kept staring at me as I read this story was when the boy got sick, and the dad referred him to his mum. The mum carried him from the morning, tending to him, till noon when he died. I asked myself, why didn't the dad stop everything he was doing for some hours to attend to his son? Was he so busy that he didn't consider the health of his boy?

I do not have additional scriptures to call this dad an uncaring father, one who considered his business more important than the health of his child and family. More so, fathers are a great blessing. I know because I'm one. So I'll leave the dad's action alone for now. But what is apparent here is the power of a mother's love.

While on this part of the story, the Holy Spirit dropped some words in my spirit. He said, "Don't underestimate what a mother can do for her child. A mother's love can move mountains."

When the child died, she knew what to do. She was going to consult Prophet Elisha. But she wasn't going to tell her husband about the child's death. Why? Because she did not accept the death. She probably thought that telling her husband would kickstart discussions about burying the child. And she didn't want to have to deal with that. She found a way to convince her husband to allow her to go and see the prophet.

Simply put, her faith told her the child was not dead

Notice also her words in the entire situation. When asked, "What's the matter?" She would say, "It is well."

This was a woman who had just lost her son. How could she say it is well when it isn't truly well? Wasn't she lying?

The answer is no. As long as she was concerned, her child was not dead. She would not bury the child. Her faith said the child was not dead.

You can say it is well even when it doesn't look like it is. If your faith says yes, God will not say no.

DON'T BURY THAT CHILD YET

What does your child represent in this story? It could be your vision; it could be your expectation; it could be your marriage hopes; it could be a great business idea you once had.

Does it look like these precious dreams are dying or even dead from the way things appear now?

Today, I bring you a word from God: Don't bury the child yet. Don't give up on your dreams, ideas, and expectations.

I heard a heartbreaking story some time ago. It was about a man of God who fell from grace to grass and buried his child before his very eyes.

According to Apostle George Anselem, who told us the story in a ministers conference, this man was a regular guest speaker in their school. The anointing on him was evident that many of the student-Christians in his time wished they had just a portion of what he had. They marked him to end at the top in a few years.

Unfortunately, he made a grave mistake. He fell into the trap of seduction. It was not deliberate, but he let *regular Christians'* judgments, attacks, and harsh opinions prevent him from pursuing God's call for his life. He buried his **child**, his love, his ministry, his passions, and his dreams.

When Apostle George bumped into him after many years, it was a sad tale. The once vibrant preacher now stayed in the village doing odd jobs to survive and feed his children.

So sad.

How many times have we allowed the opinions and judgments of others to prevent us from chasing our dreams? We let people define us by their assessments.

It's time to stop that.

Even if you have made mistakes, I'm here to remind you today that nothing can stop you without your consent. We all make mistakes in life. Don't let your mistakes define you. Wake up from your slumber, repent of your sins and start over again. Tend your child back to life. With God, all things are possible.

Here's what the Spirit of God says: *"The child is not dead."*

Now, get up and begin to say:

- It is well with my family;

- It is well with my spouse;
- It is well with my health;
- It is well with my children;
- It is well with my business;
- It is well with my dreams;
- It is well with my faith;
- It is well with my ministry;
- It is well with me;
- It is well with my visions;
- It is well with God's call and gifts upon my life;
- It is well with my ….
- I will arise again;
- I will get better and better every day;
- Things will work out again for my good.

Hallelujah!

> *"You can say it is well even when it doesn't look like it is. If your faith says yes, God will not say no."*

8

HEALING WORDS TO COMMAND YOUR HEALTH

If you need healing, learn these powerful scripture-based declarations. Declare them morning and night. Say them immediately you wake up in the morning and when you lay in the bed to sleep. Your healing will become a reality.

NO MORE GUILT

"Bless the LORD, O my soul, and forget not all his benefits, who forgives all your iniquity, who heals all your diseases, who redeems

your life from the pit, who crowns you with steadfast love and mercy (Psalm 103:2-4).

The LORD God Almighty forgives my sins and heals my diseases.

He redeems my soul from destruction and crowns me with love and mercy.

I have inner peace and forgiveness from the Lord Jesus Christ. My spirit, soul, and body are healthy, sound, and energetic.

There is, therefore, now, no condemnation for me because I am in Christ.

I have the confidence to appear before God and receive salvation, healing, deliverance, and restoration through the blood of Jesus Christ.

I FORGIVE OTHERS

In the name of Jesus Christ, I exercise myself unto forgiveness.

I free my spirit from all hurts and offenses I have hitherto nurtured in me.

I receive grace to walk in love and tolerance.

I forgive, not because I have been begged, but because I am a child of God.

Even as the LORD has forgiven me, I also forgive anyone who has offended me, in Jesus name.

I receive deliverance from any bitterness and hurt from offenses of people.

Whatever damage has been done to my health due to unforgiveness and bitterness, I receive total healing henceforth.

From today, I decree that I am healthy, sound, and active in spirit, soul, and body.

I am abounding in love, grace, and peace.

I am rich in mercy, compassion, and charity.

I am healthy and prosperous.

GOD WANTS ME TO BE HEALTHY

Healing is the children's bread.

I am Your Child, LORD Jesus Christ, so healing is my portion.

I see myself healed, renewed, and prosperous from today because that is the Will of God for my life.

Even though I am human, full of wrong thoughts and mistakes, I do not enjoy seeing my children suffer; how much more the

Almighty God. I know that He is not happy with sickness and pains in my body.

I know that God wants me to be healed and walk in divine health.

I reject any pain and sickness fighting the plan of God for my life.

I see the hand of Christ stretched towards me for complete cleansing and renewal.

In Jesus name.

GOD LOVES ME

Jesus is the same yesterday, today, and forever.

His love and compassion remain the same.

His power and grace remain the same.

If He had mercy and compassion for others in the Bible, He also has compassion for my family and me.

If He died for me to be saved from sin, how much more will He heal me.

I declare this day that I am a beneficiary of the compassion of Jesus Christ.

Because the compassion of the LORD fails not, my health will not fail again in Jesus name.

CHRIST'S DEATH IS FOR MY HEALING AND DIVINE HEALTH

I Peter 2:24 - Who his own self bare our sins in his own body on the tree, that we, being dead to sins, should live unto righteousness: by whose stripes ye were healed.

I believe in the death and resurrection of Jesus Christ. He was wounded for my sins and chastised for my sickness.

Therefore, I decree that I am healed forever and ever.

There is no debate about the death of Christ, so there is no debate about my healing and the complete restoration of my health.

No sickness has a right over my body anymore because the blood of Jesus has redeemed me.

My body is now the temple of the Holy Spirit.

So I command every form of sickness and pain in my body to be destroyed.

I proclaim my healing and total restoration.

I HAVE AUTHORITY OVER THE DEVIL

Isaiah 54:17 - "No weapon formed against you shall prosper, and every tongue which rises against you in judgment you shall condemn. This is the heritage of the servants of the Lord, and their righteousness is from me," says the Lord.

Matthew 16:19 - "I will give you the keys of the kingdom of heaven. Whatever you bind on the earth will be bound in heaven, and whatever you loose on earth will be loosed in heaven."

....

God has given me authority over the devil and his demons through my faith in Christ Jesus.

I believe and confess that whatever I bind here on earth is bound in heaven, and whatever I loose remains loosed. This is my heritage in Christ.

Today, I speak to the demons causing pains and sickness in my body. I bind them and command them to cease in their operations.

I cast out these demons propagating sickness, pain, and weakness in my body. I command them all to leave my body and never return.

I remind these evil spirits that my body is the temple of the Holy Spirit.

It also is written that in the name of Jesus Christ, every knee must bow (Philippians 2:10).

So you evil spirits, I command you all to bow now, pack your loads and leave, in the name of Jesus Christ.

I AM EXEMPTED FROM THE AFFLICTIONS OF THE WORLD

Isaiah 60:2 - For behold, darkness will cover the earth And deep darkness the peoples; But the LORD will rise upon you and His glory will appear upon you.

Colossians 1:13 - For he has rescued us from the kingdom of darkness and transferred us into the Kingdom of his dear Son,

Psalm 91:5-9 - Thou shalt not be afraid for the terror by night; nor for the arrow that flieth by day; Nor for the pestilence that walketh in darkness; nor for the destruction that wasteth at noonday.

A thousand shall fall at thy side, and ten thousand at thy right hand; but it shall not come nigh thee.

Only with thine eyes shalt thou behold and see the reward of the wicked. Because thou hast made the LORD, which is my refuge, even the Most High, thy habitation.

Genesis 7:23 - And every living substance was destroyed which was upon the face of the ground, both man, and cattle, and the creeping things, and the fowl of the heaven; and they were destroyed from the earth: and Noah only remained alive, and they that were with him in the ark.

Ephesians 2:5-6 - Even when we were dead in sins, hath quickened us together with Christ, (by grace ye are saved) and hath raised us up together, and made us sit together in heavenly places in Christ Jesus:

....

I confess that I am seated together with Christ in the heavenly places, far above principalities and powers.

I reign and rule with Christ as a king and priest before God.

I live in dominion over sin, sickness, and infirmities.

I overcome the world.

The Blood of Jesus Christ creates a wall of protection over my life and family.

The Blood of Jesus Christ protects us from all the terrors of the night, arrows of the day, and diseases that walks in darkness.

Because I am in Christ, who is the ark of salvation and deliverance, I shall be saved and spared from the activities of wickedness in this world.

Even during gross darkness and danger, the glory of the LORD rises upon me. The light of God shines in my life, in my health, in my finances, and in my home.

I shall grow from strength to strength and from Glory to glory.

In Jesus name.

Amen.

"I have the confidence to appear before God and receive salvation, healing, deliverance, and restoration through the blood of Jesus Christ."

9

BANISH ANXIETY, WORRY, AND DEPRESSION

The Bible says that only with joy can we draw from the wells of salvation. So anything that fights joy and gladness in your heart is a sworn enemy of your destiny. Some of those things are worry, anxiety, and depression. Today, you will release yourself from these enemies and enter into the rest that God has for you.

Use these declarations to banish the spirit of anxiety, worry, and depression. Decree total restoration of whatever has been injured in your life due to fear, anxiety, and depression. Here's what the Bible says:

Isaiah 12:3 - With joy, you will draw water from the wells of salvation.

Psalms 16:9 - Therefore, my heart is glad, and my glory rejoiceth: my flesh also shall rest in hope.

Proverbs 17:22 - A merry heart doeth good like a medicine: but a broken spirit drieth the bones.

Romans 15:13 - Now the God of hope fill you with all joy and peace in believing, that ye may abound in hope, through the power of the Holy Ghost.

Nehemiah 8: 10 - …"Go and enjoy choice food and sweet drinks, and send some to those who have nothing prepared. This day is holy to our Lord. Do not grieve, for the joy of the LORD is your strength."

Declare

Heavenly Father, restore in me the joy of salvation and fill me with the spirit of praise every day.

Let the JOY OF THE LORD start to overflow from inside me from now onwards.

I command the spirit of anxiety, fear, and depression in my life to bow, pack, and leave this moment in Jesus name.

From today, I receive the baptism of joy from heaven. I am rejoicing every day, walking in victory, health, and prosperity, in Jesus name.

Amen.

"Anything that fights joy and gladness in your heart is a sworn enemy of your destiny."

10

FAVOR WORDS

Psalms 5:12 - For thou, LORD, wilt bless the righteous; with favor wilt thou compass him as with a shield.

....

I am righteous through Jesus Christ.

God will bless and compass me with favor as with a shield, in Jesus name.

Psalms 102:13 - Thou shalt arise, and have mercy upon Zion: for the time to favor her, yea, the set time, is come.

....

This is my set time for favor. God has risen to have mercy upon me. His favor will make a way for me.

---

2 Corinthians 6:2- For he says, "In the time of my favor I heard you, and in the day of salvation I helped you." I tell you, **now** is the time of God's favor, now is the day of salvation.

....

Today is my day of salvation and favor. God's kindness will speak for me everywhere I go, in Jesus name.

Genesis 39:4 - Joseph found favor in Potiphar's eyes and became his attendant. Potiphar put him in charge of his household, and he entrusted to his care everything he owned.

Genesis 39:21 - The Lord was with him; he showed him kindness and granted him favor in the eyes of the prison warden.

....

I have favor wherever I go and in whatever I do. As God was with Joseph and he had favor in every situation, so also is God with me. I have favor in every place, and in everything, in Jesus name.

DECLARATION

I declare that I have favor today and every day.

I declare that I am strong and well able to fulfil my God-given destiny.

God is fighting my battles for me. I am a victor and not a victim.

I declare that I am going forward, from glory to glory.

I declare that my light is shining, brighter, and brighter, in Jesus name.

I declare that from today, everything I touch will prosper and succeed according to the perfect will of God for my life.

I declare that I have favor with people.

I have favor with kings in high places.

I have favor with my employers and everyone I do business with.

I have favor with the government.

I have favor with my family.

I have favor in all my relationships.

I have favor round about me like a shield.

In Jesus name.

Thank You, Father in heaven, for causing everyone and everything to work for my good.

Thank You, LORD, for causing me to be at the right place at the right time.

Thank You, LORD, for causing people to want to help me.

Thank You, LORD, for blessing me with creativity.

Thank You, LORD, for causing me to make right decisions with a clear mind.

In Jesus name.

I declare today that Heaven is smiling on me and that I will have favor in everything I do.

I declare that I will be blessed in the city and blessed in the country.

I will be blessed coming in and blessed going out, in Jesus name.

I declare, according to Psalm 84:11, that God is blessing me with favor and honor, and no good thing will He withhold from me.

I declare today that God and I are a majority.

I can do all things through Christ who strengthens me.

I have favor every day, everywhere, and with everyone in Jesus name.

I declare divine remembrance for myself today.

I receive grace to be a doer of the word of God, to develop capacity, to add value to my life, to pray, to sacrifice, and to relate well with people, in the name of Jesus.

I decree that favor will speak for me in the morning, in the afternoon, in the evening, and all the days of my life.

Whatever keeps me at one spot, I break them now, and I declare that I will no longer remain at one stagnant.

n Jesus name.

Amen.

11

Declarations Over Your Finances

I decree and declare that I am prosperous in everything I do, even as my soul prospers.

I live in abundance and riches.

My barns are filled with plenty and overflowing with precious wines.

I do not lack any good thing in my life; I have in excess everything that makes life meaningful – peace of mind, finances, joy, wisdom, and divine protection.

I command to come back to me every lost opportunity, and I decree that I'm restored in every aspect of my life, in Jesus name.

Henceforth, as the scriptures say in Isaiah 60,

- *People I do not know will come on their own and support me to rebuild my walls, and their kings will serve me.*

- *My gates will always stand open, they will never be shut, day or night, so that people may bring me the wealth of the nations.*

- *Where I was earlier forsaken and hated, God will empower me to become an everlasting pride and joy of everyone and all generations.*

- *I will enjoy the prosperity of nations and be invited to dine with royalty.*

- *Instead of bronze, I will be brought gold, and instead of iron, I will receive silver.*

- *Violence will no longer be heard in my abode, nor ruin and destruction within my borders.*

- *What others struggle to receive shall come to me without effort, for the Lord is my everlasting light and glory. He will show me how to excel effortlessly where others are struggling*

- *My days of sorrow are over. My sun will never set again, and my moon will decline no more because God is now my everlasting light*

- *We shall build global enterprises. The least person in my family will become a thousand, the smallest a great nation.*

God daily loads with benefits. I am blessed every day. I give and share with others, and I never lack, in Jesus name (Psalm 68:19).

I carry a divine magnet that commands others to favor me. I prosper in health and wealth. My gifts and skills open doors unto me and bring me before kings and nobles. (Proverbs 18:16)

From this day forward, my clients and customers prefer me, because my work and business are anointed, and the finger of God is upon me, in the name of Jesus Christ.

From now onwards, I am empowered to lend to nations, and I will not borrow.

The curse of debt is broken off my life in Jesus name.

Nothing dies in my hands; instead, I prosper in whatever I lay my hands.

The heaves are open unto me; I will walk in supernatural prosperity all the days of my life, in Jesus name.

> "I command to come back to me every lost opportunity, and I decree that I'm restored in every aspect of my life, in Jesus name."

12

DECLARATIONS OVER YOUR MIND

I HAVE A SOUND MIND

2Timothy 1:7 - For God hath not given us the spirit of fear, but of power, and of love, and of a sound mind.

Declare

In the name of Jesus Christ, I decree as an ambassador of God's Kingdom and representative here on earth, I have a sound mind because God did not give me the spirit of fear, but of power, of love, and of a sound mind.

I HAVE THE MIND AND TONGUE OF THE LEARNED

Isaiah 50:4 - The Lord God hath given me the tongue of the learned, that I should know how to speak a word in season to him that is weary: he wakeneth morning by morning, he wakeneth mine ear to hear as the learned.

Declare

God has given me the mind and tongue of the learned. He has empowered me to know how to speak a word in season and out of season to those that are weary. His light shines upon my head; there is no darkness, shadow, or confusion in my mind from this day forward.

God instructs my heart every morning with the knowledge that empowers me to become a blessing to this world, in the name of Jesus Christ.

I STOP FALSE IMAGINATIONS

2 Corinthians 10:3-5 - ₃We are human, but we don't wage war as humans do. ₄We use God's mighty weapons, not worldly weapons, to knock down the strongholds of human reasoning and destroy false arguments. ₅We destroy every proud obstacle that keeps people from knowing God. We capture their rebellious thoughts and teach them to obey Christ (NLT).

Declare

I cast down the strongholds of human reasoning and mental calculations that limit me in life. I wear on the cloak of God's thinking and mindset henceforth.

I command to be destroyed every false argument, philosophy, imaginations, and every high thing that exalts itself against the knowledge of God in my mind, and I arrest rebellious thoughts and declare them subject unto the obedience of Christ

---

I THINK LIKE GOD

Genesis 1:26-27 - ²⁶ Then God said, "Let us make human beings in our image, to be like us. They will reign over the fish in the sea, the birds in the sky, the livestock, all the wild animals on the earth, and the small animals that scurry along the ground."

²⁷ So God created human beings in his image. In the image of God, he created them; male and female, he created them (NLT).

Declare

I am a duplicate of divine knowledge.

I have access to God's way of thinking.

I am in charge of the affairs of life

I am creating and re-creating my world

As God spoke and everything was created, so I speak, and what I say comes to pass

I am creative; I create things that solve problems in the world.

Because I interact with God, instructions will not depart from me.

God shows me unusual mysteries of life, and my thoughts align with the intelligence of the Almighty.

Through the wisdom of God, I transform spiritual mysteries to real-world commodities.

I stand where God has positioned me, and I access the secrets of creation and dominion.

My heart is encouraged, motivated, and inspired, and ready to pursue and establish things the Almighty commands.

I create systems, influence systems, and upturn evil systems.

My mind is empowered by God to decode hidden secrets, heavenly protocols, and spiritual procedures that command earthly matters to align to my favor.

Through my thoughts and my words, I create eternal things, powerful things, precious things, wonderful things, righteous things, prominent things, profound things, and God things.

I declare that my God-nature is active and working now and always. When I speak, my words stir holy passions in others to do what is just.

As I serve God and promote His plan, God honors me. He takes me to places that my certificates, my qualifications, my background, and my capabilities cannot take me.

Though I am an earthen vessel, God houses treasures in me. I decree that these treasures will be recognized and celebrated in this generation.

Every divine investment in me is converted from potential to purpose. All parts of my life begin to flow out the resources of the heavenly.

In the name of Jesus Christ. Amen.

IT'S MY TIME TO MANIFEST

Romans 8:19 - For all of creation is waiting, yearning for the time when the children of God will be revealed (VOICE).

Declare

I declare that I was born for such a time as this. Through the Holy Spirit in me, I key into heaven's prearranged agenda for man on earth today. I am participating in the fullness of God's lavish grace and power for this time. Going forward, I will manifest His dominion in all spheres of life.

I am an extension of God's power and prophetic mandate.

From today, the things God causes me to accomplish on earth will be so visible and enormous that His name will be glorified wherever I am found.

I am a full extension of the Godhead. I am empowered and helped by the Spirit of God. I have dominion over the works of the flesh. I will no longer fulfil the lusts of the flesh because I ride on wings of divine power.

I am like Jesus and as Jesus in this generation. I speak the language of influence and command proven results in the works of my hands. I work miracles through my hands and exemplify the fullness of divinity, in Jesus name

I ACCOMPLISH IMPOSSIBLE THINGS

Luke 1:37 - For with God nothing shall be impossible.

Genesis 18:14 - Is anything too hard for the Lord? At the time appointed, I will return unto thee, according to the time of life, and Sarah shall have a son.

Declare

I declare that I am an embodiment of grace. I am helped by God every day to represent Jesus in my place of work. Through my thoughts, words, and actions, the kingdom of God is advancing, and the kingdoms of hell are disintegrating.

I declare that my spiritual gifts are refired daily; my Christian character grows daily; my principle is deepened daily, and my possibilities are stretched continually.

I am blessed and empowered every day. Things considered impossible before now are henceforth possible before me because I carry God, the impossibility specialist.

I heal the sick, raise the dead, work miracles, and stop the mouths of lions. This is what Jesus asked me to do, and that is what is happening with me. I am blessed because I come in the Name of the Lord.

I declare that I am following a divine plan for my life. I go where God sends, and I do what He asks. I give what He requires, and I take what He provides.

I am enjoying divine comfort and provisions. I am living in God's abundance. My life is reflecting the benefits of a King's child.

The power of the divine life is activated over me. I have an unquestionable capacity to produce beyond human capability, in Jesus name.

Amen.

13

DECLARATIONS OVER YOUR LIFE

In the name of Jesus Christ,

I declare that I can do all things through Christ who strengthens me.

I declare that my relationship with God grows deeper and deeper, and my love grows more and more unto the perfect day.

I receive an abundance of grace and the gift of righteousness. I reign in life through Jesus Christ (Philippians 4:13, Romans 5:17).

I declare that my relationship with my spouse is fitting in the Lord. My spouse loves, cares, and protects me, just as Christ loves, cares, and defends his church. Our hearts are united and bound in love and perfect understanding towards each other, in Jesus name.

I declare that I am kind and tender-hearted toward others. I forgive as the Lord forgave me. I do not concern myself with my interests alone. I look out for the interests of others (Ephesians 4:32, Philippians 2:4).

O Lord, set a guard over my mouth and watch over the door of my lips. Cause me to speak when necessary and make my words a token of healing and comfort for those who hear me, in Jesus name (Psalm 141:3).

I declare that God's peace that passes understanding rules my heart. When storms arise in any way, my heart will be calm, my spirit will be at rest, and my access to divine order and instruction will be unshaken, for God is always with me. He will never leave me nor forsake me.

I declare that I walk in a manner worthy of the Lord, pleasing Him in all respects. I bear abounding fruits of righteousness in every good work, and I am increasing in the knowledge of the Almighty God.

His power strengthens me and empowers me to endure and be patient until my change manifests (Colossians 1:10-11).

I declare that God takes pleasure in my prosperity. As I learn and meditate on the Word of God day and night, I prosper supernaturally, and everything I lay my hands excels beyond the explanations of men (Psalm 35:27, Psalm 1:2-3, Joshua 1:8).

I declare that God makes all grace abound toward me so that I always have all sufficiency and abundance in every good.

Because I honor the Lord with my giving and with my first fruits, my barns will be filled with plenty. My tanks will overflow with new wine (Proverbs 3:9-10).

I declare that I prosper in all things and I abound in good health even as my soul prospers (3 John 1:3).

I declare that I am redeemed from all kinds of curses because Christ redeemed me from the curse of the law by becoming a curse for me.

I enjoy all blessings as I serve and obey the Lord my God.

I am blessed in the city and blessed in the country

I am blessed in the fruit of my body.

I increase in my herds, my cattle, and the offspring of my flock.

I am blessed when I come in and blessed when I go out

I declare that the LORD causes my enemies who rise against me to be defeated before my face; when they come against me in one way

God causes them to flee before me in seven ways.

The LORD commands His blessing on my storehouses and in all that I set my hand to do, and He blesses me in the land that He has provided for me to stay.

I declare that the Lord has established me as a holy person to Himself. He reveals His ways to me and empowers me to keep His instructions.

All the people of the earth will see that I am called by the name of the LORD.

I will be fruitful in the fruit of my body, in the increase of my livestock, and the produce of my ground.

The LORD opens to me His good treasure, the heavens to give the rain to my land in its season and to bless all the works of my hand

I will lend to many nations, and I will not borrow.

The Lord makes me the head and not the tail; I will be above only and not beneath.

(Galatians 3:13, Deuteronomy 28:1-13)

I declare that the God of hope fills me with all joy and peace in believing so that I abound in hope by the power of the Holy Spirit.

The Lord of peace is my peace. In every way, He always gives me His peace (Romans 15:13, 2 Thessalonians 3:16).

I declare that the joy of the LORD is my strength. I am confident of this very thing, that He who has begun a good work in me will complete it until the day of Jesus Christ

God works in me both to will and to do His good pleasure (Nehemiah 8:10, Philippians 1:6, Philippians 2:13).

I declare that I hold fast to the word of life. In the day of Christ's return, I will have reason to glory because I will not run or labor in vain (Philippians 2:16).

I declare that I am anxious for nothing, but in everything, by prayer and supplication with thanksgiving, my requests will be made known to God. And the peace of God, which surpasses every human knowledge, will guard my heart and my mind in Christ Jesus (Philippians 4:6-7).

I declare that I choose to meditate on whatsoever that has virtue and is praiseworthy. My mind will only think about things that are true, noble, just, pure, lovely, and of good report (Philippians 4:8).

I declare that I willfully forget the past; I forget everything behind and reach forward to things that are ahead.

I press toward the goal for the prize of the upward call of God in Christ Jesus; I press on daily, and in the name of Jesus Christ, I will lay hold of that which Christ Jesus has also laid hold of me(Philippians 3:12-14).

I declare that God instructs me and keeps me as the apple of His eye every day. I am a crown of glory and a royal headband in the hand of the LORD. God rejoices over me as a bridegroom rejoices over his bride (Isaiah 62:5).

I declare that I speak pleasant words that are sweet to the soul and healing to the bones. I am wise, and I bring healing. I have a health-giving tongue which is a tree of life to myself and others (Proverbs 15:4, Proverbs 11:30, Proverbs 18:21).

I declare that God redeems my life from the pit. He crowns me with His loving-kindness and compassion. He satisfies my mouth with good things and renews my youth like the eagles' (Psalm 103:3-5).

I declare today that sadness, depression, frustration and every other vice of the devil is far from me because I have total trust in God and I depend on Him completely. I will be still, and know that He is God. He will be exalted in all areas of my life (Psalm 46:10)

I decree according to God's word that two are better than one, because they have a good reward for their toil. For if they fall, one will lift up his fellow. Therefore, I call forth God-sent, destiny friends and helpers, who will help me achieve God's plans in my life as I help them too, in Jesus name (Ecc 4:9-12, Psalm 27:17)

SOMETHING GOOD IS ON YOUR WAY

GET IN TOUCH

We love testimonies. So, please share how this book or other of my books has inspired or helped you. Connect with me on social media:

Facebook: www.facebook.com/drdanielokpara

Instagram: @drdanielokpara

Telegram: https://t.me/mybetterlifetoday

Also, please consider checking out my other books on Amazon:

amazon.com/author/danielokpara .

Visit our website, www.BetterLifeWorld.org, and send us your prayer request. As we join faith with you, God's power will be made manifest in your life.

BOOKS BY THE SAME AUTHOR

LATEST BOOKS

Prayers to Cancel Disappointments at the Edge of Breakthrough

Prayers to Cancel the Curse of Marital Delay

Prayers to Remove Yourself from Negative Generational Patterns

31 Days in the School of Faith

31 Days With the Heroes of Faith

31 Days With the Holy Spirit

31 Days With Jesus

31 Days in the Parables

None of These Diseases

I Will Arise and Shine

Psalm 91

ALL BOOKS

Prayer Retreat:
HEALING PRAYERS & CONFESSIONS

- 200 Violent Prayers
- Hearing God's Voice in Painful Moments
- Healing Prayers
- Healing WORDS
- Prayers That Break Curses
- 120 Powerful Night Prayers
- How to Pray for Your Children Everyday
- How to Pray for Your Family
- Daily Prayer Guide
- Make Him Respect You
- How to Cast Out Demons from Your Home, Office & Property
- Praying Through the Book of Psalms
- The Students' Prayer Book
- How to Pray and Receive Financial Miracle
- Powerful Prayers to Destroy Witchcraft Attacks.
- Deliverance from Marine Spirits
- Deliverance From Python Spirit
- Anger Management God's Way
- How God Speaks to You
- Deliverance of the Mind
- 20 Commonly Asked Questions About Demons
- Praying the Promises of God
- When God Is Silent
- I SHALL NOT DIE
- Praise Warfare

Prayers to Find a Godly Spouse
How to Exercise Authority Over Sickness
Under His Shadow

AUDIOBOOKS

120 Powerful Night Prayers that Will Change Your Life
28 Days of Praise Challenge
Anger Management God's Way
By His Stripes
Deliverance of the mind
Healing Words: Daily Confessions & Declarations
How God Speaks to You
How to Exercise Authority Over Sickness
How to Meditate on God's Word
Prayers to Find a Godly Spouse
Praying the Promises of God
Take it By Force
Under His Shadow
When God Is Silent
Besides the Still Waters
Less Panic More Hope
How to Pray for Your Family
Prayers that Break Curses
20 Commonly Asked Questions About Demons

Deliverance by Fire
Command Your Money

ABOUT THE AUTHOR

Daniel Chika Okpara is an influential voice in contemporary Christian ministry. His mandate is to make lives better through the teaching and preaching of God's Word with signs and wonders. He is the resident pastor of Shining Light Christian Centre, a fast-growing church in the city of Lagos.

He is also the president and CEO of Better Life World Outreach Center, a non-denominational ministry dedicated to global evangelism, prayer revival, and empowering of God's people with the WORD to make their lives better. Through his Breakthrough Prayers Foundation (www.breakthroughprayers.org), an online portal leading people all over the world to encounter God and change their lives through prayer, thousands of people encounter God through prayer, and hundreds of testimonies are received from all around the world.

As a foremost Christian teacher and author, his books are in high demand in prayer groups, Bible studies, and personal devotions.

He has authored over 50 life-transforming books and manuals on business, prayer, relationship and victorious living, many of which have become international best-sellers.

He is a Computer Engineer by training and holds a Master's Degree in Christian Education from Continental Christian University. He is married to Doris Okpara, his best friend, and the most significant support in his life. They are blessed with lovely children.

WEBSITE: www.betterlifeworld.org

NOTES

Printed in Great Britain
by Amazon